Cool
SCHOOL
DRAMA AND
THEATER

Karen Latchana Kenney

A Division of ABDO

ABDO
Publishing Company

visit us at www.abdopublishing.com

Published by ABDO Publishing Company, a division of ABDO, P.O. Box 398166, Minneapolis, Minnesota 55439. Copyright © 2011 by Abdo Consulting Group, Inc. International copyrights reserved in all countries. No part of this book may be reproduced in any form without written permission from the publisher. Checkerboard Library™ is a trademark and logo of ABDO Publishing Company.

Printed in the United States of America, North Mankato, Minnesota
112010
012011

 PRINTED ON RECYCLED PAPER

Editor: Liz Salzmann
Series Concept: Nancy Tuminelly
Cover and Interior Design: Anders Hanson, Mighty Media, Inc.
Photo Credits: Anders Hanson, Shutterstock, Thinkstock

The following manufacturers/names appearing in this book are trademarks: Aleen's® Tacky Glue®, Clean Colors® Rich Art®, Duncan® Scribbles®, Elmer's® Glue-All™, Fiskars®, Sulyn Industries Glitter Glue

Library of Congress Cataloging-in-Publication Data

Kenney, Karen Latchana.
 Cool school drama and theater : fun ideas and activities to build school spirit / Karen Latchana Kenney.
     p. cm. -- (Cool school spirit)
 Includes index.
 ISBN 978-1-61714-668-8
 1. Drama in education. I. Title. II. Title: Cool school drama and theater.
 PN3171.K358 2011
 372.66--dc22
                        2010024870

Contents

What's Cool About Drama & Theater?

Going to school is not just about homework and tests. You get to meet new friends and learn amazing new things. Plus, there are so many activities to do and fun groups to join.

Being excited about school is your school spirit. One way to show it is by joining a school group. What do you love doing? Can you dance or sing? Or do you like to play games or learn languages? Guess what? School groups are filled with other students who like doing the same things as you!

Drama and theater groups are really cool to join! Do you like to wear costumes and pretend to be other people? Maybe you like to read poetry or sing songs from musicals. That's all a part of drama and theater. If you want to show school spirit, a drama and theater group may be right for you!

Before You Start

It's a good idea to do some research before joining a group. Talk to people who are in drama and theater. Go to **rehearsals** and watch what goes on. See if drama and theater is right for you. Is it something that you *want* to join and *can* join?

Time

- How often does the group meet?

- How long are meetings and rehearsals?

- Are there any trips required?

Skills

- What do members do at meetings and rehearsals?

- Do I need to have special skills to join?

- Do I need to **audition** for the group?

Cost

- Do I need to pay a group fee?

- Are there any costs for trips or costumes?

Permission

Once you've done your research, check it out with your parents. Make sure you get permission to join the group. You may need a parent's help to fill out an application or registration form.

The World of Drama & Theater

What's one place you can be really dramatic? A drama or theater group! You can also show your creativity and imagination. Here are just a few ways to be part of the action.

Many drama and theater groups perform plays. In a play, there are different acting **roles**. Students **audition** for the roles. Then the director decides who should play each role. Like plays, musicals also have many roles. But singing is a big part of a musical production.

There are theater games and exercises that can help you practice. You can work on your acting style and character **development**. Share ideas with group members. You will learn from each other and grow as actors!

If you don't like to perform, you can still be part of the fun! Sets need to be built and costumes need to be created. Who will play the music or run the lights? It takes a whole production crew to make things look terrific onstage.

There are different kinds of drama and theater groups. See what your school has to offer. The right group is waiting for you!

Way Back

Have you heard of William Shakespeare? Probably! He is known as one of the best **playwrights** of all time. Shakespeare lived from 1564 to 1616, during the **Renaissance** period. That was a time when theater became very popular in England. Shakespeare both wrote and acted in plays. Today, his plays are still performed on stages around the world.

Tools & Supplies

Here are some of the materials you'll need to make the projects in this book!

2-inch
mini-canvases

strip magnet

paint

puffy paint

ribbon

jewels

ruler

paintbrushes

pen

pencil

markers

highlighters

empty container

canvas tote bag

poster board

scissors

white paper

colored paper

scrapbooking scissors

glue

glitter glue

What's Your Role?

Can you imagine the fun you'll have in drama and theater? **Audition** for a part onstage. Or get involved backstage. There are many things that need to be done besides acting!

What can you do to take part in the fun? Join a drama and theater group and see what you like best. If you want to act, you may have to **audition** for a **role**. You can act a scene or sing a song. Then the director will give you a role.

It takes more than actors to put on a performance, though. Costumes and sets are needed. Music and lights need to be added. There is usually a sign-up sheet for the non-acting ways to be involved. Remember, it takes many people to make stage magic!

Once you're in a group, help get other people to join. How can you get them to your meetings? You need to get the word out about drama and theater. Put up posters and make magnets. Find fun ways to **describe** the group's activities. New members will soon fill the extra roles!

Try, Try Again

If your audition doesn't go well, don't give up! **Rehearse** your scene. Practice in front of a mirror. Then try again at the next audition!

Magnet Mania

Spread the word about your drama
and theater group with these magnets!

What You'll Need

2-inch mini-canvases, glitter glue, puffy paint, paint, paint brushes, strip magnets, scissors, glue

1 Have the group **brainstorm** fun messages to put on the magnets. What do you love about drama? What makes theater so cool? Write down the ideas. Remember to keep them short!

2 Write the messages on the **canvases**. Use puffy paint and glitter glue. Try different colors.

3 Paint a shape around the message. Make it simple, such as a circle or a star.

4 Paint the canvas outside of the shape. Make it one color or try stripes or dots. Paint the sides of the canvases too.

5 Wait until the paint dries. Then turn the canvases over. Cut strip magnets as wide as the canvases. You'll need two magnets for each canvas.

6 Glue the strip magnets to the wood frames. Put one on the top and one on the bottom of each canvas. Your drama and theater magnets are ready!

Fun With the Troupe!

Lights, music, action! Did everything work out? It takes a team to pull off a production. Can your group work together? That's the fun of teamwork!

It takes communication to make a performance run smoothly. There are many things that need to be in place. Sets and costumes need to be finished.

The lights and sound effects need to be set up. The actors have to know their lines. The whole group needs to **rehearse**. Then problems can be worked out together.

A drama group can spend long hours preparing for a performance. But it is also important to work on team building. You can make crafts together or play fun games. Try starting with the next activity. You could throw a cool party. It will help your group grow closer and help the new members feel not so new!

Make a commitment to get to know the people in your group. Show your **appreciation** for their hard work. Your performances will improve as the group grows closer. Being friends will also make opening night more fun!

Funny Props

At your next party, why not play a theater game? It's a fun way to break the ice. Put different props in a box. Try a piece of fabric, different hats, and some weird glasses. Pass the box around and have each person pick a few props. Then you can each make up a funny character. Everyone will laugh as you act for each other!

T-E-A-M-O!

Learn about the people in your group with this fun game!

What You'll Need

white paper, scissors, colored paper, glue, pen, ruler, markers, empty container, highlighters, cool prize

1 Trim the edges of a sheet of white paper. Glue it to a sheet of colored paper to make a border. Divide the white paper into squares. There should be at least as many squares as there are players. Make a card for each member.

2 Have everyone sign a square on every other member's card. Remind them that they can only sign each card once! If there is an empty square left over, write *free* in it.

3 Write each club member's name on a strip of paper. Put the names in the container.

4 Have the group president or a teacher draw names. When each name is called, that person stands up. He or she tells a fact about himself or herself.

5 Everyone draws an X on that person's name on their cards. Use highlighters so the names are still readable. As names are called, more squares will be marked off. The first person to have a line marked off shouts, "Teamo!" Give him or her the cool prize!

To Be Seen, or Not To Be Seen!

You have to advertise your performances to get a crowd, right? Make posters and banners. And don't forget your logo! It will help fans know who's putting on the show!

What does your drama group do? Put on plays or musicals? Or maybe you perform comedies or read poetry. What you do is part of your group identity. And a great way to show it is by creating a group logo.

A logo is something that can be used on posters, banners, and other printed pieces. It is a symbol that represents a group. Logos can have pictures and words, and the colors are important too.

The following activity will help you create a logo for your group. Be creative and make it look great. Then use it in different ways to represent your group!

Using Your Logo

When your logo is finished, scan it into the computer and save it as a picture. Use a document program to make things with your logo.

- Add it to letters

- Put it on flyers

- Print it on T-shirt transfer paper

If you can't use a computer, use a color copier. Make your logo as big or small as you want. Put it on banners, posters, and signs.

Make sure to keep the original logo safe. You'll want to use it again!

Produced by the Stage Gang!

Put your group's stamp on posters and banners with a logo.

What You'll Need

pencil, paper, markers

1 Start with a **brainstorming** session with your group. Ask questions such as *Should our logo have a theme? What words or letters should be in our logo? What picture should be in our logo? What colors should be in our logo?* Write the ideas down.

2 Go through the list with the group. Vote for the best idea for each question and circle it.

3 Now, sketch out your idea. Decide what shape you want your logo to fit inside. You could start with a stage! Draw that shape on a piece of paper.

4 Put the picture and words inside the shape. You might need to make several sketches. Move the picture and words around. See what works best. Remember to keep it simple!

5 Show the sketches to the group. What do they think? Pick out the logo that everyone likes.

6 Now make a final sketch on a new piece of paper. Make the lines clear and sharp. This will help it look good whether it's printed big or small.

7 Color your logo with markers. Use only a few colors. The colors should look clean and bright.

Time to Play Your Part!

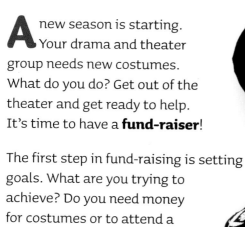

A new season is starting. Your drama and theater group needs new costumes. What do you do? Get out of the theater and get ready to help. It's time to have a **fund-raiser**!

The first step in fund-raising is setting goals. What are you trying to achieve? Do you need money for costumes or to attend a play? Set your goal and then figure out how much money you need.

How are you going to raise funds for your group? There are many things you can do. You can have a garage sale or a car wash. You can also sell tickets for a special **fund-raising** performance. **Brainstorm** ideas with the group and talk with your director. There may be costs to put on your fund-raiser. Include the amount you spend when deciding how much money you need.

During your fund-raiser, be friendly and show **appreciation**. Let people know how their money will help the group. They will be happy to help the drama and theater group achieve its goals!

Do's and Don'ts

Do

- Listen to everyone's brainstorming ideas.

- Thank people for helping!

Don't

- Goof off during a fund-raising event.

- Be disappointed if you don't reach your goal.

Buy a Star!

It's fun to see your name up in the school halls.

What You'll Need

poster board, pen, scissors, colored paper, scrapbooking scissors, glitter glue, markers, tape (optional)

1 Get permission before hanging anything up in school hallways. Ask the principal or a teacher. Find out if it's okay to use tape on the walls. If not, ask what you should use instead.

2 Make a stencil for your star shape. Draw a star on the poster board. Then cut it out.

3 Trace the star onto colored paper. Draw as many as you can on each piece. Use different colors of paper.

4 Cut out the stars. Try using scrapbooking scissors to make fancy edges.

5 Write "_____ is a drama star!" on each star. Add glitter glue around the edges. Make cool designs with markers too!

6 Sell the stars. You could charge 25 cents or 50 cents for each one. Have the buyers write their names on the lines. Hang the stars up in the halls. Everyone will know they are drama stars!

Drama in Action!

It's time for the big performance! Don't forget to bring your costume to the theater. Use this fun bag and your school spirit will show!

Theater Tote

A cool way to carry your drama and theater stuff!

What You'll Need

scrap paper, canvas tote bag, puffy paint, ribbon, scissors, fabric glue, jewels, transfer paper (optional), iron (optional)

1 Cover your work area with scrap papers or a large sheet of white paper. Set out your materials.

2 Lay the tote bag out flat. Use puffy paint to write the name of the group. Put it in the middle of the bag. Make the letters big.

3 Add your name to the bag in one corner. Use a different color.

4 Now add a fun trim! Cut a piece of ribbon as wide as the bag.

5 Squeeze a line of glue along the top edge of the bag. Press the ribbon onto the glue. Make sure it is straight!

6 If you want to add an image, now is the time! It should be about you and the drama group. For example, you could draw theater masks.

7 Time to add some bling! Glue jewels onto your bag. Add a few here and there.

8 You could add your logo to the bag! Print it on transfer paper. Find a good spot for it on your bag. Then ask an adult to iron it on.

9 Wait until the bag is dry. Flip it over and decorate the other side. What a cool tote bag!

Conclusion

What do you love about drama and theater? Is it the cool people you met? Or is it performing in front of an **audience**? Maybe you love being creative and using your imagination. There are so many things that are great about being in drama and theater groups.

It is a way to support your school. And you meet people who like the same things as you. It's a great way to make friends and have fun. You get to achieve goals and participate in many different activities. This can help you become more confident outside of drama and theater.

Drama and theater groups are cool ways to show your school spirit. But they are not the only way. Check out the other books in this series. Learn about clubs and groups you can join at your school. Maybe you like to volunteer or play games. Or learn languages or play music. There will be a club or group that fits your tastes. Take advantage of what your school has to offer. It is a great place to be!

Glossary

appreciation – the feeling of greatly valuing or admiring someone or something.

audience – a group of people watching a performance.

audition – 1. to try out for a role in a performance 2. a meeting where an actor tries out for a role.

brainstorm – to come up with a solution by having all members of a group share ideas.

canvas – a piece of cloth that is framed and used as a surface for a painting.

describe – to tell about something with words or pictures.

development – the act of growing, changing, or improving.

fund-raise – to raise money for a cause or group. A fund-raiser is an event held to raise funds.

playwright – a person who writes plays.

rehearse – to practice a performance. A rehearsal is a meeting where a performance is practiced.

Renaissance – a revival of art and learning that began in Italy during the fourteenth century.

role – a part played by an actor.

Index